TRAINING AFRICAN GREY PARROTS
KW-025

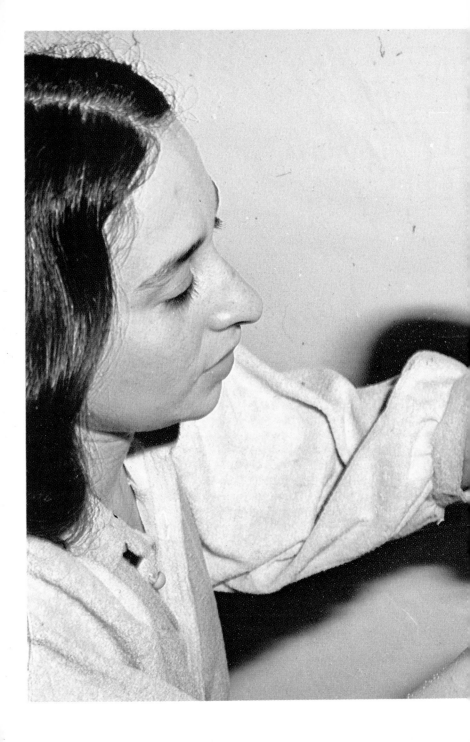

Contents

Photographers: Glen Scott Axelrod, Dr. Herbert R. Axelrod, Tom Caravaglia, John Daniel, Sam Fehrenz, Harry V. Lacey, Max Mills, E.J. Mulawka, San Diego Zoo, Louise van der Meid, Vogelpark Walsrode.

Overleaf: The author, Risa Teitler, working with an African grey parrot. **Title page:** African grey parrots are extremely intelligent birds which, when tamed, make wonderful pets.

Distributed in the UNITED STATES by T.F.H. Publications, Inc., One T.F.H. Plaza, Neptune City, NJ 07753; in CANADA to the Pet Trade by H & L Pet Supplies Inc., 27 Kingston Crescent, Kitchener, Ontario N2B 2T6; Rolf C. Hagen Ltd., 3225 Sartelon Street, Montreal 382 Quebec; in CANADA to the Book Trade by Macmillan of Canada (A Division of Canada Publishing Corporation), 164 Commander Boulevard, Agincourt, Ontario M1S 3C7; in ENGLAND by T.F.H. Publications Limited, Cliveden House/Priors Way/Bray, Maidenhead, Berkshire SL6 2HP, England; in AUSTRALIA AND THE SOUTH PACIFIC by T.F.H. (Australia) Pty. Ltd., Box 149, Brookvale 2100 N.S.W., Australia; in NEW ZEALAND by Ross Haines & Son, Ltd., 18 Monmouth Street, Grey Lynn, Auckland 2, New Zealand; in the PHILIPPINES by Bio-Research, 5 Lippay Street, San Lorenzo Village, Makati Rizal; in SOUTH AFRICA by Multipet Pty. Ltd., 30 Turners Avenue, Durban 4001. Published by T.F.H. Publications, Inc. Manufactured in the United States of America by T.F.H. Publications, Inc.

TRAINING
AFRICAN GREY
PARROTS

RISA TEITLER
PROFESSIONAL TRAINER

Introduction

One of the most desirable attributes of pet parrots is their talent for mimicry. A truly good talking parrot is a source of pleasure and pride for the owner. The African grey parrot, or grey parrot, is one of the most gifted talking birds and can acquire an extensive repertoire of words, music and sounds. They learn quickly and, in addition, can be very affectionate towards their owners. They are active birds and spend much of the day climbing around, whistling, talking and playing.

These parrots are native to equatorial Africa, where they live in large flocks, roosting together in the same trees nightly. Their natural foods include seeds, nuts, berries, fruits and vegetables. They have been known to descend upon corn crops and cause considerable damage, but they reportedly spend most of their time feeding in the treetops.

African grey parrots are tiny when hatched, but they soon grow to a length of approximately 13 inches, although size can vary greatly from bird to bird. The plumage is predominantly gray with a scalloped effect. Feathers of the head, facial area and rump are pale gray, while the back, chest and abdominal feathers are darker gray. In some birds the entire body may be more silver than gray, often due to regional differences. Flight feathers are black, as are the bill and feet. In

The tail feathers of the African grey parrot are bright red in color, while the rest of the plumage varies in shades of grey.

An African grey parrot and an Amazon parrot. Although Amazon parrots are usually good talkers, the African grey is considered to be superior in both voice and ability to acquire a large vocabulary.

startling contrast, the tail is bright red. Very young birds display a dark gray iris that turns yellow as they mature.

There are three subspecies of the grey parrot. Two of these, *Psittacus erithacus erithacus* and *Psittacus erithacus princeps*, are quite similar, but the latter is restricted to a few islands in the Gulf of Guinea, and its plumage tends to be dark gray. The third subspecies, *Psittacus erithacus timneh*, has a maroon tail edged with reddish brown. The upper mandible is reddish with black tip; the lower mandible is black. The timneh is generally smaller in size than the other two subspecies and is found in only four West African countries: Guinea, Sierra Leone, Liberia and the western region of Ivory Coast. The timneh is rarely seen for sale. All three subspecies make equally good pets, and their life expectancies are the same. The grey parrot is a long-lived bird and may live for 40 to 50 years. There is, however, very little documented data on the life expectancies of grey parrots.

Left: When approaching a new bird for the first time, offer it a stout stick upon which to perch. *Below:* Do not offer your hand to a strange bird, as it may bite you in self-defense. Wait until you have become better acquainted.

Personality

When buying an African grey parrot, be prepared to spend some money. Due to their remarkable capacity for speech, African greys command higher prices than some of the Amazon parrot species.

The great majority of grey parrots come from Africa with their wings already clipped. This is extremely unfortunate. During the long period of time spent in transportation and quarantine, with the birds living in close quarters, the clipped feathers tend to fray and split. In some instances the quills break down to the skin line and may cut the edge

of the wing. If the edge of the wing is severely cut, damage to the feather follicles may occur, and the bird may never regrow proper flight feathers. Be certain to examine the clipped wing before purchasing the bird.

A pet grey parrot is best left as a single bird. Two birds are unnecessary unless you are considering a breeding experiment. The single bird will tame down faster and acquire speech more readily. Do not be concerned with the sex of the grey parrot you buy as a pet; both males and females make fine pets. Personality is much more important than sex. Look for a bird that is alert and watching you as intently as you are watching it. Remember that African greys are high-strung birds, and don't be put off if the birds on display all run to the corner of the cage and squeeze together. This is normal behavior. Greys often hang off the top of the cage and emit a crying, growling sound when frightened. Again this is normal behavior and should not be the basis upon which you reject a bird. The great majority of African greys growl at their new owners until they begin to feel secure in their new environment. Even tame African grey parrots will growl at strangers or anything else that upsets them.

African greys are extremely intelligent birds. They are versatile and usually adjust quickly to changes in routine or environment. What should you expect from the African grey? Initially, it may be nervous and cry constantly. If you spend plenty of time with the parrot, it will soon calm down and begin to watch you carefully, noting every move that you make. This is one reason that you should learn to move slowly and deliberately around the new parrot. The grey will listen intently to your voice and to all household noises, dogs, cats, bells, buzzers, television and more.

The way that you behave with the wild bird will determine its response. You can give the bird self-confidence by having it yourself. Remember that you are the most important influence on your bird's personality development. If you are nervous when handling the bird, the emotion will undoubtedly be transmitted to it.

There are a couple of basic personality types worth discussing, but don't attempt to fit your pet into one of these catagories. Personality typing is meant only to help you set up the right kind of taming and training regime. Obviously, you cannot expect to handle every grey parrot the same way and achieve the desired result. Some greys are quiet, steady birds that never growl. These individuals are often tamed to sit on your hand in just one lesson. As soon as you present your hand, they lift one foot and step on. These birds, of

The personality of the African grey parrot will differ from bird to bird; in addition, the personality of the grey will be affected by that of its owner.

course, are the most desirable pets and can usually be taught any number of tricks as long as the trainer is consistent with his lessons.

Another type is the steady but growling bird. These birds also are often easily tamed, but your eardrums may take a beating until the parrot gets used to you. Keep in mind that the bird is just expressing itself. Whatever you do, don't walk away from its cage or stand just because it is growling. If you do that, you may teach the bird that you'll leave it alone if it growls at you long and loud enough. This is one of the most common errors that an inexperienced trainer can make.

Another personality type is the frantic bird. These greys will run from you and never try to make eye contact with you. They are very difficult to get out of the cage and often refuse to sit on a stand, jumping off and running away in any direction. These are hard birds to tame and require much more time and effort on the part of the trainer, but by no means should you consider such a bird untrainable. This is the most common excuse that a person can give for running out of patience with a grey parrot. With a frantic grey you must work close to the floor in a very small area. It is extremely important to protect these parrots from injury by padding the floor and taking other extra precautions, such as moving the cage into the training area and placing it on the floor, instead of trying to get the bird out of the cage from a table top or stand. If necessary, open the cage door and go away until the bird comes out by itself. Then go in, remove the cage from the training area and work very, very slowly with the bird. Talk to it, sing to it and, above all, don't frighten it. You may want to corner it on the padded floor and slowly move your hand over to touch the bird lightly on the back or wings. Never hit this type of bird for biting. It is

Below: Push the stick gently under the bird, forcing him to perch upon it. **Opposite:** Do not mistake a soft, gentle nip for a vicious bite. African greys frequently mouth their owners' hands harmlessly.

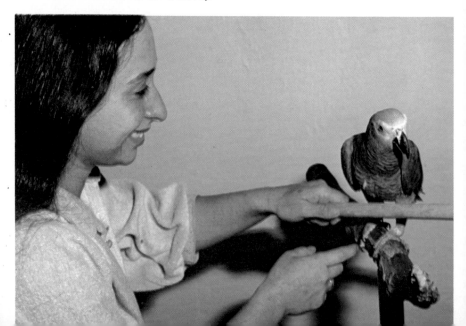

already terrified of humans—don't confirm its fears. Birds like this usually don't try to bite you; they are more concerned with escape. So work slowly and patiently. Tailor your lessons to give the bird confidence in you, and be prepared to spend many days, perhaps weeks, winning the bird over. If you follow this advice, you will eventually have a very tame pet and the pleasure of knowing that you accomplished the task.

The last type that will be discussed here is the biter. Grey parrots can indeed inflict a painful bite when they want to. With biting birds, you may be forced to use some hand and arm protection during the first few taming sessions. Use lightweight, skin-tone gloves, not heavy garden gloves, or the bird will think of you as the same person who grabbed him so many times during capture, shipping, and quarantine. Wear a lightweight jacket. If you have long hair, tie it back. Take off rings and other jewelry that will attract his attention. Again, work these birds in a small area so that you don't have to chase them around if they should run from you. Before offering your hand, work them first with a stick until they learn to step on without hesitation. Use your voice, saying "No" loudly to stop a biter from biting you. Give this bird plenty of time, at least one month, before you decide that its biting can't be cured. If after many lessons you still can't change this

behavior, try to find someone with more experience to train the bird for you. You may want to ask the shop that you purchased it from to trade you a different bird, and sell this one to a breeder. Examine the alternatives before you condemn the grey parrot to a life in the cage. Don't label your new grey parrot a biter if it bites you once or twice. Put yourself in the bird's position. Wouldn't you show your anger and fear by trying to hurt the giants who have hurt you so much since you were captured?

As I said before, don't automatically put your bird into one of the categories described. Just use them to try to arrange a proper taming and training regime for your new African grey parrot.

The adjustment period has stages. Within one month, the grey should be fairly calm and begin to relate to you more easily. After six months, the grey will be a part of your daily routine and you a part of its. It should have acquired a few words by then, or household noises if it hasn't had speech lessons. It should be hand-trained and may enjoy having its head scratched. It will wait anxiously for you to uncover it and feed it in the morning, and may call you if you are late getting up. It will also look forward to your returning from work in the afternoon to let it out of its cage. After two or three years, the bird's vocabulary could be fantastic, and if you continue to teach, it will

The newly acquired African grey parrot will go through various stages of adjustment with its new owner. Patience and understanding will go a long way in helping the bird acclimate itself to its new home.

continue to learn. African greys have very good memories.

African greys have some natural fears that you should keep in mind. Fast movements and loud, sudden noises are going to frighten them. Until your bird is used to you, it may be afraid of your hands or fingers. If this seems to be the case and the bird is afraid of your fingers, tuck them under your palm when trying to tame it. If it reacts adversely to the curled hand, try a flat hand, with fingers held together as though you were going to karate chop something. You may try touching the bird with one finger. Its responses to you must shape your approach to taming and training. A new bird is often afraid of cage doors, stepping onto your hand only to jump off as you try to maneuver it out of the cage. Try coaxing it out with food, or try getting it out on a stick. You may

have to stand back and just wait for it to come out by itself. The bird's confidence in you will grow as a function of time.

Some greys exhibit real affection for their owners. When a grey parrot is handled exclusively by one person, it may become very jealous of any other person or pet that interferes in the relationship. Jealous behavior should be avoided by proper training. In other words, unless you want a one-man or one-woman bird, be sure that more than one person attends to the bird daily. Even so, an individual grey, like many other parrots, may seem to be more fond of women than men or more fond of men than of women. The African grey is a highly emotional, intelligent

*Opposite: A pet shop proprietor with an African grey parrot. Your local pet shop is a good place to look for an African grey. **Below:** Pet shops feature many products which will help you keep your African grey in good health and pleasant surroundings.*

parrot and is not recommended as a pet for young children.

African greys can be housed in either indoor or outdoor aviaries. Most often they are kept inside the house. A cage for the single bird must be large enough for it to have ample exercise when left alone in the daytime. You should not clutter its living space with too many toys, swings, perches or feeders. Both indoor cage and outdoor aviary must be constructed of metal, not wood. For outdoor aviaries, one-inch by one-inch or two-inch by one-inch welded wire is fine.

The outdoor cage must be constructed to offer shelter from the weather, especially rain and wind, or the bird will eventually succumb to illness. The bottom of all cages should be easy to clean. Outside, a foundation of cement covered with a thick cushion of wood shavings will serve this purpose. Newly acquired birds should not be placed into outdoor aviaries in which they might suffer injuries from falling to the ground before the flight feathers grow in enough to enable flight. Continually striking the ground can cause both internal and external injuries and possible death. One-inch by one-inch or two-inch by one-inch wire mesh is a good choice for construction of the outdoor facility. Wire of smaller mesh can cut the bird's feet when it climbs around or hangs from the side or the top of the cage. Wire

having a larger mesh size invites escape and allows rodents to enter freely.

There must be plenty of sunshine in the aviary, but African greys must be protected from the strong, burning rays of direct sunlight. If the cage top is not adequately shaded by surrounding trees, don't use a solid metal sheet to cover the cage. Too much heat gathers in the top of solid metal covers and may burn or dehydrate the birds. Ideally, there should be both wire and solid portions to the cage top.

Greys are very hardy when fed and housed properly, and some people keep them outside even in winter. If possible, have ample facilities indoors in case of very cold weather or severe winter storms. In some parts of the world, hurricanes are a seasonal threat. If you live in a hurricane area, don't leave the bird to weather the storm outside.

An African grey will thrive in a stable environment as either an aviary or household bird. Indoor pets should have a bird stand in addition to a cage. The majority of single pets are kept with their wings clipped, making the bird stand an indispensable item. Your bird can travel freely from room to room and even outside with you if you train it to remain on a stand.

Occasionally you may encounter an African grey in a lawyer's office, flower shop, hardware store or other business

Whether you house your African grey parrot in an outdoor aviary or in a cage, be sure its environment is safe and stable.

establishment. Many greys adjust to life as store birds, but they should never be teased or frightened. These working birds should not be left on an open stand 24 hours a day. They deserve a secure cage to roost in at night. If you plan to keep your bird in a business establishment, make certain that it is out of the mainstream of traffic, behind your desk or counter. Never chain the African grey to a bird stand. This is unnecessary, inhumane and dangerous.

Left: Stick training is the first stage of the taming process. *Below:* Once you have trained your grey to perch on a stick whenever it is offered, you can then substitute your hand for the stick.

Taming the African Grey

A GOOD TRAINER

The African grey is not a pet for young children; therefore, the taming of a grey parrot should never be left to a child. Both men and women are equally good at taming as long as they have adequate time and patience to devote to the task. A good trainer must have self-confidence and be able to recognize the cues that stimulate the bird to respond favorably to the training sessions. A well-structured lesson is the responsibility of the trainer. In order to shape the bird's behavior positively, daily handling is very important. You will get poor results

from a bird that is handled one day and ignored for two or three days. A good trainer will work with the bird each and every day.

People who habitually lose interest in special projects should not attempt the taming or training of a grey parrot or any other bird. A nervous or anxiety-ridden person is a poor choice for a bird trainer. If your schedule is very busy, you had better leave the taming to someone else, for the bird's benefit.

Only one person should do the initial taming with an African grey parrot. The trainer needs a cool head so that he doesn't drop the bird or strike it if it bites him. Most likely the bird will try a few bites before he is tame, so be sure that you understand the possibility of being bitten. If this prospect frightens you terribly, let someone else accomplish the task of taming.

TAMING

Before beginning, make sure that you have all of the necessary equipment. A bird stand, preferably a low one; three sticks, a long one and two short ones (one-inch diameter); pads for the floor; and a few food rewards should be available. If training is to be done in a carpeted room, you

An African grey on a perch that is provided with feed cups. Food, as a reward, is an important part of the bird's training process.

Before beginning the taming session, be sure to have a prepared area containing all the necessary equipment.

won't need the pads for the floor. A bird net can be very handy if the grey gets into an inaccessible place, but don't use the net unless you have no other way of retrieving the bird. After all, you are trying to tame the bird, and continually netting him is not going to win him over. If you have never tamed a bird before, you may want to invest in some tight-fitting cotton gloves or a pair of golf

gloves in a neutral shade; birds are usually frightened by gloves, so stay away from bulky or colorful ones. Dispense with the gloves completely once you feel confident with the bird. If possible, try to accomplish the task without using any gloves at all. You may find that the bird doesn't care to bite you anyway. Grey parrots are usually not aggressive and bite only when they are frightened, not

Steps in training your African grey: Using a stout perch, force the bird to step onto it. Keep at it until the bird steps onto the perch. If the bird withdraws its foot, keep trying. Hold the stick lower if the bird hesitates to step too high. Pet the bird and talk to it gently after it has succeeded. Gently raise the stick off the floor. Now try to get the bird to perch on your hand. Next, move the bird from perch to hand, then from one perch to your hand and from your hand to another perch. Try to have the bird on your hand and the perch at the same time. When you've completed this training, you will have a well-trained bird ready for further instruction.

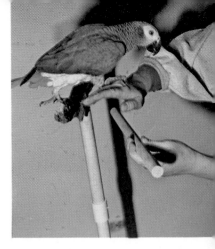

to be mean. Move slowly and deliberately so as not to frighten the bird, talk to give it confidence and it may not try to bite you even once.

The taming area should be as open as possible to allow freedom of movement and to protect the grey from colliding with hard objects. Therefore, a carpeted or padded floor is very important. Cover mirrors and large glass windows or doors. Work in a quiet area by yourself. The presence of more than one person will scare the bird and distract the trainer.

The best candidate for taming is a young bird (a gray cast to the eye indicates youth) with good plumage and no exposed blood feathers on the clipped wing. The bird must be in good health and eating well before you begin taming. Taming exercise may be too strenuous for an undernourished or ill bird.

As the trainer, you must learn to observe the bird's behavior. This observation should begin before you purchase the bird. The behavior of African greys is best observed with a single individual specimen, but in pet shops you usually see three to ten individuals in a cage. Step back to avoid inhibiting the birds, and watch them carefully. Don't buy the poor little fellow that the others trample over. Choose the best physical specimen and observe. Does it sit quietly on the perch while the others jam into the corner? Does it

make eye contact with you and follow your movements? When you approach slowly, does it run away excitedly, or does it cautiously back away? Does it have a steady or nervous appearance? (Constant moving from side to side and bobbing of the head indicate nervousness.) Since African grey parrots are often high strung, the steady bird that makes eye contact with you and reacts cautiously is a better candidate for taming. An older bird with yellow eyes should not be rejected if it meets the criteria outlined above.

You may purchase a bird with full wings, but this is unlikely. If the wings are unclipped, make sure that the job is done properly. Learning to clip the wing by doing it is foolish. If you lack ample experience in watching or assisting in this procedure, have a vet or bird handler help you.

Don't clip both wings. Look at them and leave the better feathered wing alone. To clip the wing you will need sharp scissors, a pair of small wire cutters, good light, styptic powder in case of accidents, and a person to assist you.

Restrain the bird by wrapping it in a towel or, if you feel capable, hold it in your hands. Catch the bird in a net or towel. Remove its feet first and hold them firmly but gently with one or two fingers between the legs. Give your

African grey parrots will growl when they feel threatened. This behavior is perfectly natural and will be overcome when the bird feels secure in its new home.

assistant the feet to hold while you get the bird's head. A word of warning here: many greys have long necks and can easily twist out of your hand, so follow directions carefully! Place your thumb under the lower mandible and support the head and neck with your other fingers. Use two hands to hold the bird. Once the feet and head are out of the net, either give the holder the bird or, if you are holding, be certain that you have the feet and head securely before beginning. Think over what you are going to do to

be as fast as possible. Hold the head straight and don't pull or push on the neck or feet. Support the bird on your towel-covered lap or padded countertop. Holding the bird out in mid-air invites accidents. Extend the wing gently, holding it firmly at the wing bend. Look for any blood feathers (feathers that have not fully grown in), and be certain not to cut these feathers. If you cannot readily identify blood feathers, don't clip the bird. If you can identify them, don't clip away the feathers on either side, leaving the blood

Right: How you buy your bird is most important. Never buy a parrot from people who don't know parrots. Visit your local pet shop first. *Below:* The owner of the shop will usually handle the bird for you. *Opposite, top:* Have the pet shop owner show you how to handle the bird properly. *Opposite, bottom:* Your local pet shop will most likely carry a selection of bird books that you will find most helpful.

feathers exposed, or you are taking a chance on breaking them during taming. There may not be any blood feathers present; this is the ideal situation.

Leave the first two feathers and cut the next two in half with scissors. Now take the wire cutters. Push back the underfeather coverts with your finger to expose the feather shafts. Clip off the next ten feathers where the feather begins to emerge from the shaft. Leave at least ¾ of an inch of feather shaft emerging from the wing to protect it from injury. Clip the wing from the inside, not the outside. After you are done clipping, place the bird on the floor to give it an opportunity to discover its inability to fly. Let this sink into its head before you lift it off the floor.

You may want to clip the claws at the same time you clip the wing. Holding the bird in the same manner as before, the holder should give the person who is clipping room to maneuver from one toe to the next. Use the wire cutters to tip each claw, and be certain not to clip the nail off too short. You must have styptic powder on hand in case of accidents. Again, if you lack expertise, let the vet do the clipping for you. Always work in good light, thinking over the procedure before beginning, and working as quickly as possible. File each claw with a nail file after you finish clipping them all.

In some instances the claws may become badly overgrown. Cut off a little at a time to avoid hitting blood. If you should hit blood, stop and medicate with styptic powder before going on to the next nail. Take the styptic powder and press it against the bleeding spot with your finger. Make sure that bleeding has stopped before you continue. If bleeding is very bad, use dry cotton to press against the styptic powder. When bleeding has abated, put the bird back into its cage and let it heal for a day or two before you handle it again.

Now that the manicure is complete, get down to the business of taming. Place the bird on the floor and train it to step onto a stick. Work low to the floor. Place the stick in front of the bird and push gently against the bird's body. Once it steps on, wait a minute and place it back on the floor. After a few minutes of drill with the stick on the floor, place the grey on a low stand (two to three feet high). Remember, pad the floor. Practice having the bird step from the stand to the stick and back again. Work for a few minutes and let it rest a minute. Continue this type of drill until the

Opposite: Natural wood perches will help wear down the bird's claws and will help exercise the bird's feet. If the claws need clipping, however, be sure to have someone experienced show you the proper method.

bird automatically steps onto the stick when it is presented. Now replace the stick with your hand. The bird may step onto your hand immediately. If so, keep it there and stand very still, talking to the grey. Place it back onto the stand after a few minutes and continue to drill the bird in this manner until it steps onto your hand without hesitation. The grey parrot is too large to train to a finger; use your whole hand.

If the bird tries to bite you, tell it "No" in a loud voice and move your other hand to distract it, but don't draw away. If you draw away, the grey will know that it can scare you. Don't hit the bird for biting you. Scold it soundly and learn to use your free hand to distract it from biting. If the grey persists in trying to bite, spend some time giving bits of food from your fingers. Drip water onto its beak with your hand. Let it get used to your hands. Be patient and use your common sense. Keep all of your attention on the bird. Some birds step onto your hand, sit there a minute and then bend down to bite. If you are

The best way to train your parrot is to utilize several short sessions a day. Try to be aware of the moods of your bird; when it starts to get tired, put it back in its cage for a rest.

A well-trained African grey can be taught to play "dead" and to perform many other tricks. However, be sure the bird has mastered the basic requirements for tameness before moving on.

attending to the task, you should be able to stop such a bite before it makes contact with a strategic "No" and some distracting movement of your free hand.

Train the bird to step onto your hand and back onto the stand before you consider walking around with it. Use your voice to reassure it throughout the sessions. Speak in low, soft tones and use its name often. Reward it with bits of food as a part of every lesson. The grey may take the

reward and toss it into the air for a while, but eventually it will learn to take it graciously.

For advanced speech training it is imperative that your African grey take food rewards, so you may as well begin that training immediately. Most greys have very good appetites, so you shouldn't have too much trouble getting your bird to take food from your hand. Try seed, peanuts and some different fruits and vegetables to find out what your bird likes the most. Use the bird's favorite food to motivate it in any taming or training lessons.

Once the grey is fluently stepping from the stand to your hand and back again, teach it to step from one hand to the other. Do this slowly. Each time you work with the bird (hopefully more than once a day), review the entire lesson—stick, hand and perch training. You will soon be able to dispense with the stick completely.

It is not advisable to attempt to hand-train a grey parrot inside its cage. Birds are very possessive of their own cages and tend to bite more readily when tamed in this manner. In addition, by leaving the grey inside its cage, you will soon discover its amazing ability to avoid you by climbing around on the top, sides and bottom of the cage. Let the bird come out of the cage by itself if it won't come out on a stick. Eventually it will step out onto your hand readily, looking forward to the freedom that tame birds enjoy. Some birds need only one or two lessons before you can consider them tame. Others take a long period of time. If you are highly motivated and work each day with the bird, it will soon come around to your way of thinking. Some birds are so nervous that they continually jump away from you at every opportunity. The trainer must draw on every bit of patience and know-how that he has in these situations. Work close to the floor for a longer

period of time before placing the bird on a stand. Make certain to use a low stand to protect the bird from falling too far to the floor. Learn to use your body to block escape routes. Offer food, water, patience and frequent lessons. A determined trainer reaps the benefits of his work.

Other problems in training the bird may appear. Many greys insist upon climbing up your arm to your shoulder and then to your head. This is fine once the bird is tame enough to step onto your hand from your head. Many greys like to ride on their owners' shoulders wherever they go. It is important to teach your bird to remain on your hand when you are doing the initial taming. If the bird tries to climb your arm, use your free hand to block it. Put your hand in front of the bird in a vertical position. This usually works to keep the bird where you want it.

If after eight weeks of dedicated work at taming your new grey it is still not responding to you in the desired way (the desired way being not biting, stepping onto your hand, taking food from your fingers), review your taming sessions carefully. Do some serious thinking. Have you been working with the bird consistently, or only sporadically? Be honest with yourself. Remember that some birds are harder to tame than others. Even a tame bird may not become your best friend for six

Wild-caught or imported African grey parrots may have a fear of bulky gloves. Therefore, if you must use gloves for the taming sessions, be sure to use tight-fitting gloves rather than heavy gardening gloves.

months to a year. Give the bird plenty of time and a good routine to help it adjust. Above all, don't try new and dramatic approaches to taming, such as wetting the bird or working him in a totally darkened room. The change from one method to the other will undoubtedly confuse the grey and, not knowing what to expect from you, it will begin to distrust you.

The taming methods described are not the only way, but they have proved successful with many African grey parrots. Daily lessons, repetition, sincere effort and patience are the most reliable principles in taming.

A Good Training Routine

The first hour after you get the new bird home is very important. Arrange to spend the first full day at home with the bird. Place it in its cage to settle down or, if you are really motivated, take it out in the prepared training area and begin immediately. Spend one hour in the first taming session. You may spend time just talking to the bird, but for some nervous or older birds this is important. Don't think that you are wasting time; you aren't.

After the first lesson, you may spend anywhere from 20 to 60 minutes in each lesson. It is not suggested that you spend every minute making the bird do something. It will need to rest once in a while, and so will you. The two of you resting together is important in the scheme of things. You will soon learn to be comfortable together, and the grey will demonstrate that it is at ease by cleaning its feathers while you sit close, watching. Observing a grey parrot or any other bird at close range is one of the most enjoyable pastimes you can imagine.

Let the bird out of its box or cage low to the padded floor. Speak to it in low tones. Move slowly. Offer it bits of food. Use a stick to teach it to step up from the floor or bird stand. Have a low stand (two to three feet high) to begin perch training. Make the transition from stick to hand as soon as possible. Practice having the grey parrot step from the stand to your hand. Try to touch the bird's breast once it seems calm enough to allow it. Try petting it on top of the head. Move very slowly when attempting to touch the bird. Be patient and have confidence in yourself as a trainer.

For working people, a good routine includes cleaning and feeding the bird in the morning before work. Use this time to talk to the grey. If possible, give yourself a few minutes to try touching the bird in its cage. Don't get the bird excited, but if it climbs up and hangs off the top of the cage, try stroking it with your finger. If the bird sits on its perch when you open the door, offer it a peanut or piece of raw corn. A bird that jumps around the cage and growls needs more time to listen to your voice and watch you as you move around doing the morning chores. It will soon learn to adjust to your lifestyle. Before walking out the door for work, be certain to address the bird and say "Goodbye" or "Bye-bye."

When you get home in the afternoon, set up your schedule to allow ample time for handling the

Opposite: A good training routine will help you tame and train your bird more quickly. Nevertheless, you should never allow your bird to be unsupervised; in addition, it is a good idea to keep your bird indoors.

bird outside of the cage. This is the time for intensive training. In between the short sessions, let the grey rest on the stand and get used to the freedom of being outside the cage. Consider that imported birds have gone through a long period of confinement with many other birds. It is interesting to watch them adjust to having free time outside the cage. They soon learn to love their new-found liberty and will yell and whistle at you until you take them out in the afternoon. You may find it convenient to allow the bird to remain on the stand all evening, giving it short lessons and putting it into the cage when you are ready to retire for the night. It is advisable to give the grey parrot plenty of structure in its new environment. Birds react in a positive manner to structure and

At some point during the training process, your bird may attempt to climb onto your shoulder or onto your head. It is a good idea to wait until both of you are familiar with each other before you allow the grey to do this.

Occasionally, pink feathers are seen in the plumage of an African grey parrot. This characteristic has been arousing the interest of breeders in recent times.

routine. Cover the cage in cold weather. Cover it halfway in warm weather.

If you are fortunate enough to be at home in the daytime, your training with the bird can progress more rapidly. Take it out in the morning before feeding, and place it on the stand where it can see you and you can keep an eye on it. Be sure to place the stand in a spot that won't be disturbed by normal household activity. Go through your regular routine, making time for a few short taming lessons throughout the morning. This is the ideal time to teach the grey parrot to eat from your hand, and later for speech training. Place the bird back into the cage if you plan to go out shopping or leave the house for any period of time. Remember to offer the bird a drink of water now and then. Take your grey out again in the afternoon before the other family members arrive home. Repeat the taming procedure. Keep in mind that the bird may tame down slowly and give it at least two to three months before you decide that it is untrainable. Growling is normal behavior for the grey and should not be considered as a sign that the bird is wild. It may be as sweet as you could wish for and still growl. Before allowing other people to handle your parrot, make sure that the bird is fairly fluent in stepping from stand to hand and back again. Many grey parrots allow one person to handle them and no others. Avoid this by allowing other family members to handle the bird once it is tame. Keep in mind, however, that young children should never handle the bird without supervision. Even after a discussion of the proper method of handling, you may decide that your child is too young to handle the bird. If so, follow your instincts as a parent. Both the grey and the child are depending on you for guidance. Birds are not toys for children, after all, and many can be too rough for a child to play with.

Below: If you own more than one bird, be sure to keep your new grey separate until it has been tamed and until the birds have become accustomed to one another. *Opposite:* Many fanciers consider the African grey to be the most majestic of all parrot species.

Advanced Speech and Trick Training

Once you have accomplished the task of taming the grey, you will probably consider going on to advanced training. First, let us review the characteristics of a tame bird. The tame grey should not bite you without provocation. (If you grab a bird and it bites you, it has had just provocation.) It should step up onto your extended hand without hesitation. It should step from hand to hand, from stand to stand and from stick to hand readily. It should be taking bits of food from your fingers, even if it throws them into the air instead of eating them. It should sit on its stand without jumping off at your approach. If something frightens the grey, making it jump to the floor, it should still be willing to step onto your hand when you offer it. The tame bird will not necessarily let you pet it, but many enjoy being touched. Growling may not stop immediately when the bird is hand-tame, but the growls should be considerably softer in volume and will eventually be emitted less often. The tame bird should be willing to venture out of its cage when you open the door, even if it won't step out onto your hand. Once the bird is outside the cage, have it step onto your hand and transfer it to the stand.

Now that we know the behavior to expect from a tame individual, we are ready to discuss further training. Training differs from taming in that the individual bird has already mastered the basics. The trainer is now attempting to modify the bird's behavior beyond the basics of taming. With African greys this often takes the form of speech training. It does not matter whether you have a male or female grey. Both have an excellent capacity for speech and tricks. A young bird will learn faster than an older bird, but this does not mean that a four-year-old bird is too old to learn.

SPEECH

There are many approaches to speech training that you can employ. If you talk to the bird in the morning as you go through your regular routine before work, the bird will learn to speak very well. Unfortunately, it will not learn to speak on command by this method of training. Command speech refers to the bird's saying what you want it to say when you want it to say it. For example, the bird should repeat after you. If the word is "Hello," the bird should respond immediately after you utter the word. Birds that speak on command are amusing and can keep you entertained for hours.

Opposite: Although older African greys are not untrainable, it is easier to begin with a young bird whose dark eyes have not yet turned yellow.

If you have decided to put in the time necessary to train the grey to speak on command, you must have at least one lesson a day; three or four short lessons are better still. Take the grey out of the cage and let it sit on the stand. The bird must have learned to take food rewards from your fingers. If this has not been accomplished, change the feeding time from morning to afternoon and do your training before it gets the big meal of the day. If you work, divide the daily amount of feed in half and give half in the morning, do your training in the afternoon and feed the remainer in the evening. Never skip the bird's meal entirely. By so doing, you invite illness. If the grey is very stubborn about taking food from your hand, give just a small amount of feed in the morning and save the rest for the evening. To repeat, never withhold the food altogether. Changing the feeding time will accomplish the task without endangering the bird's health. Most greys have voracious appetites and learn to eat from your hand easily. Try sunflower seeds, peanuts, corn kernels, bits of fruit—whatever your grey likes the most.

Always have an ample supply of food rewards when you do speech training. Be prepared to give the bird its reward immediately; don't make it wait for you to pick the reward up out of a cup. Immediate reward for the desired behavior, in this case verbalization, is the most important factor in training the bird to speak on command. To begin, tell the bird, "Hello, (name of bird)." Repeat every few seconds. Make eye contact with the bird. Reward the bird for any sound that it makes at first. You must first reward for verbalization and then work closer and closer to the sound "Hello." Hello is a two-syllable word, and you will begin to notice that the bird will make a two-syllable sound to copy you before it comes out with a definite "Hello." After it gets the first word, continue to drill the bird in the same way until it is fluent with it. Remember to reward for every correct response. You can go on to new words or short phrases after the grey gets the first word. Do not try to teach the grey two different words or phrases at once, or you will confuse it and prolong the learning process.

Build the grey's vocabulary from single words to short phrases to long phrases and melodies and so on. For example, first teach "Hello, (name of bird)." Then, "How are you?" or "Hi, sweetie." Later you could try "How about a peanut?" or "Gimme a kiss, honey." If you want to teach melodies, choose a section of a song that you can sing to the bird accurately. Remember, it will learn to copy you, so if you sing off key, so will the bird. Don't try to teach a whole song at once. For example, choose a song like

Several types of parrot playpens are available at pet shops. These sets will amuse you and your bird for hours. Be sure, however, not to crowd the bird's area or cage with too many toys.

"Farmer in the Dell." Just use the part, "The farmer in the dell, the farmer in the dell, hi ho the derry, oh, the farmer in the dell." This is a real mouthful for any bird, but it can be accomplished.

Many short lessons are better than one long lesson. A ten-minute speech lesson is quite enough for bird and trainer alike. Give as many ten-minute lessons as you can each day, but leave enough time in between for the lesson to sink in. A five-minute lesson is no waste of time. If that is all you can devote, give three or four five-minute lessons.

Don't work with the television or radio in the background. This will add too much outside stimuli to the lesson. Try to work in a quiet room, but there is no need to put out the lights or close the curtains. Morning hours are good ones for speech training, and so are the later afternoon hours. Sunrise and sunset trigger the bird's natural desire to vocalize, so use this to your advantage.

Recorded speech lessons work, but the bird will not get used to the cue of having a person in front of it when it speaks. If you have absolutely no time for training the bird to speak, you probably have no time to play with it either. In this case, don't get yourself a bird. It will be lonely and unhappy. Use a recorded lesson if you want the bird to sit inside the cage and talk, but don't expect the same results as from a live lesson. Recorded

A bird stand is very convenient, as it allows the bird a place to perch while it enjoys the liberty of being outside of its cage.

It will probably take quite a while before an African grey feels confident enough to lie down in its owner's hand. However, with patience and understanding, your pet can learn to feel this confident with you.

lessons are available at retail pet shops, or you can make your own on cassette tape. There is no need to cover the cage when using a recorded speech lesson.

There is a difference between imitative and responsive speech. Imitative speech refers to the bird's repeating after you. Responsive speech refers to the bird's saying a phrase to coincide with what you have said, but not the same words. For example, you say, "How are you?" The bird responds, "I'm fine." Or you say "What's your name?" and the bird says, "Freddie." Response speech is more difficult to accomplish, but it is very

interesting and adds real depth to your bird's training.

To train your bird to use response speech, first teach the correct answer ("I'm fine"). When your bird says this without hesitation, begin to ask the question, "How are you?" Reward for the correct response, in this case "I'm fine."

TRICKS

African greys can be taught to do many things. Begin with simple tricks like waving. Touch the bird's foot and, when the bird lifts the foot, provide a reward. Give the grey the same type of lessons that you would for speech training—

many short lessons every day. Immediately reward for correct response.

Teach the bird to lie on its back in your palm. Of course the bird must first have learned to let you pet it. Don't force the bird into lying on its back, or it may give you a nasty bite. Work slowly and don't expect your bird to learn this behavior in a week or two. Remember to reward whenever you work with it. Once it has learned to lie on its back, try teaching it to roll over.

Greys can be taught to climb ladders and ring a bell at the top. Provide your bird with a small piggy bank and toy money to drop through the coin slot. Make a small wagon for it to load up and pull down a runway. African greys have a great variety of natural behaviors. Observe the bird at

It is a good idea to fasten your African grey's cage door with some sort of lock, as parrots are very clever and may be able to free themselves when you are out of the room.

It is most important that the owner of an African grey be confident and consistent when training the bird. The proper attitude will go along way in instilling confidence in the pet parrot.

play and use its natural antics when deciding what to teach as a trick. Work on only one trick at a time. Reward immediately for the desired behavior. Ignore the undesired behavior. Use many short lessons every day. Before beginning, provide yourself with the needed props and a good training area. Work in the same place in the same manner each time. Don't expect the grey to perform for others until it has completely mastered a given behavior.

Buying an African Grey Parrot

There are a few possible sources from which to purchase an African grey parrot. Look around at the local retail pet shops and see what is available. If there are no grey parrots in the shop and the proprietor offers to have a bird shipped in, consider that you will be buying the bird sight unseen. It is far better to see the bird and examine it before making the purchase. Go to all of the reputable retailers in your area and compare the asking prices for untame as opposed to tame birds if offered. Use your eyes and nose to determine whether the shop is a clean one. If the cages are dirty or the water or feed dishes fouled, it is best to look for another seller.

You may be fortunate enough to buy a grey from a private individual who purchased the creature and ran out of patience or perhaps never had any to begin with. These birds are often well fed, and the risks of buying a bird in poor health are fewer. If the bird is offered for sale with the cage, be sure that it is adequate, or purchase another. Keep the cage, however; extra cages often come in handy. If you are lucky enough to locate a breeder of African greys, call and inquire whether there are any for sale. The breeder can offer you a top quality bird, but be aware that he will ask for a top quality price for it. Remember that you get what you pay for in the bird world. A hand-fed baby grey is a prize indeed. If

at all possible, get one.

Once you have located the source, observe all the greys offered for sale. Don't let the pet shop employee make the choice for you. If the birds are housed in separate cages, move from one to the other and observe. If they are all in one cage, spot one that appears to be in good feather and observe how it behaves in relation to the others. A bird that makes eye contact with you has a good self-concept and is a good choice for taming. If it sits quietly (not listlessly) on the perch watching you, and moves slowly away as you approach, the bird is a good choice for further examination.

Eyes must have an alert look (a dull cast may indicate an unhealthy condition) and must not have any swellings or tearing. The facial skin should be free of scales and sores. (A small scratch is nothing to worry about.) The nasal openings must not be dirty, clogged, red, runny or irregularly shaped. Plumage should be smooth and even all over the body. If the feathers look chewed, don't let anyone tell you that it is because it is a baby bird. This is

Opposite: Be sure to examine your potential pet parrot for any signs of ill health. A healthy bird should have clear eyes, bright plumage, and an interest in its surroundings.

just not so. Young birds should have the same even plumage as older birds. Don't buy a bird with bare spots. If the tail feathers are absent, examine the area closely when the pet shop employee takes the bird out of the cage. If there are new feathers growing, no problem. If there is no evidence of feather replacement or there are lumps on the tail area, don't buy the bird.

Closely examine the clipped wing. Most of the grey parrots come from Africa with the wings already clipped. So be certain that there is no extensive damage to the edge of the wing. If there are sores, areas of dried blood, lumps or swellings, reject the bird or be prepared to take it to a good vet right after purchasing it.

Look at the droppings on the cage bottom, and look at the bird's

When you approach the cage of a newly imported African grey, do not be alarmed if the bird tries to run away from you. This action indicates that the parrot is aware of what is going on around it.

The place from which you purchase your African grey should provide the birds with clean surroundings and fresh food. In addition, although the shop's cages will be more crowded than those for pet parrots in someone's home, the bird should have some room in which to move around.

vent. If droppings are bright green, all white or very watery, you may be purchasing a sick bird. Droppings from a healthy bird are both dark green and white and have solid form. If the vent is soiled, red or distended, reject the bird.

Before you have the pet shop employee grab the bird, observe its respiration. Don't buy a bird with irregular, rapid or labored breathing. Birds breathe from their chests, not from their throats, and a bird whose throat palpitates with each breath should be rejected. A healthy bird has a slow, even respiration.

Once the bird is removed from the cage, examine its feet and toes. If it is missing one claw or even a toe, this is not a problem unless there is evidence of soreness or recent injury. Feel the bird's chest. A thin bird with a protruding breastbone is undernourished and should not be purchased. Some grey parrots have prominent breastbones. As long as there is plenty of meat on either side of the breastbone, you can buy the bird without worry. Decide for yourself whether the bird has enough meat on his bones—don't let the seller decide for you.

A grey that passes all of these tests is most likely a healthy specimen and a good purchase. It is not unwise to have the bird examined by a good bird vet even if it does appear healthy. Have a stool sample checked for parasites. Also have the doctor look at the clipped wing and listen to the heart. There is no reason for him to take a blood sample, however, and as the the the bird's owner you should inquire about all such procedures to protect your pet from unnecessary stress.

Transport the bird in a closed box or covered cage. This will protect it from drafts and keep it from jumping around and injuring itself. You should not transport the bird if it is raining. By doing so, you endanger the bird's health. If you want a particular bird, pick it out and have the shop hold it in a separate cage (you will probably be purchasing one anyway) until the weather improves.

Cages should be made of metal, not wood. Stay away from cages with plastic tops and bottoms. Don't buy a large parakeet cage; the wire is too thin and spaced too close together. You must accommodate the

grey's large feet with standard heavy parrot wire. If the wire is painted, it will not be as easy to maintain in good condition. The dimensions of the cage should be no smaller than two feet high and 20 inches square. A bottom grill is recommended to facilitate cleaning and to keep the grey out of its own droppings. The cage must have at least two cups; some come with four, and this is ideal.

The door must be large enough for the bird to come out onto your hand without touching the sides. It must also have a sturdy latch to keep the bird inside. You would be wise to invest in an additional latch or lock, for greys are usually great escape artists. You'll be amused and bemused to find them opening up the door at will.

A swing will provide the grey with a nice place to roost for the night or for a daytime snooze. The perches should be wooden, not plastic, with a diameter of one inch. There is no need to cover the perches with sandpaper. Natural wood perches are the best that you can provide. Ask your pet dealer whether he has manzanieta branches, or try to obtain a well-dried piece of oak. Periodically you may have to replace the grey's perches if it chews them up, but look at it this way: better the perches than the feathers.

Greys are avid chewers. If you provide them with chewing material like small fresh branches, they will usually keep from

All furnishings for the parrot's cage, such as toys and feed dishes, must be sturdy enough to hold up to a parrot's beak.

chewing their perches. Clean the perches and the swing periodically with sandpaper or a perch scraper to keep them free of residues.

Feed dishes must be parrot-sized. You will find that most of them are made of hard plastic. You can purchase ceramic dishes if you prefer, or metal; but whatever the material, be certain to clean the water dish daily with hot water and soap, and the feed dishes every few days. You will need one dish for water, one for seed and one for gravel. The seed dish can also be used for the grey's fruit and vegetables, or use another cup if you like.

You can buy or make a variety of toys for the bird, but don't crowd its cage. Add toys slowly so that the bird will appreciate them. After all, your main objective should be to have the bird play with you, not a bunch of toys. Don't give the bird a mirror. This will make the task of taming and speech training harder. Bells are fine, as long as the clappers are secure. Ladders can be used most effectively outside the cage. Inside they tend to get very dirty. Give the bird a good heavy chain to chew on. Thin chains are too dangerous. Your pet dealer may carry bird playgrounds. These are fine, but don't let the bird spend all of its time outside the cage playing in the playground or training will not progress satisfactorily.

You will need at least one bird stand (two are twice as good), a low stand 2½ to three feet high for initial taming, and a higher stand four feet high for the bird to sit on once the taming is complete. Training sticks also come in handy. They should be one inch in diameter.

Cages and stands can be plain or ornamental, as long as they are easy to clean and serve the purpose for which they are meant. You may want to invest in a smaller cage to use for transporting the grey or as a hospital cage in case of illness.

Below: Always supervise any interaction between your African greys and other pets. *Opposite:* If you intend to house two or more birds in the same area, be sure to provide enough perches.

Feeding

You should feed the bird a good fresh sunflower seed or parrot mix as the staple items of diet. Parrot mix comes with dried corn, peanuts, pumpkin seed, some oats and hot red peppers. If you use plain sunflower seed, add three or four raw unshelled peanuts each day. Also provide parakeet seed, which contains oats, and supply fresh peppers now and then. Buy your feed from your pet shop or a farm supply. Feed purchased at the market has been sitting on the shelf too long. Give your bird a dog biscuit (small size) or purchase monkey chow from the pet shop.

In addition to the seed mixture, provide fresh fruit and vegetables every day. Raw corn on the cob, green beans, peas in the pod, squash, apples, citrus fruits, bananas, peppers and tomatoes are just some of the items that your grey parrot might enjoy. There is no need to give it all of these items every day. A good rule to follow is one green and one yellow vegetable, a slice of citrus and any other fruit each day, in addition to the seed mixture. In addition, provide the bird with a fresh green leafy vegetable on a daily basis. Romaine, chickory, dandelion greens, turnip tops and carrot tops all make fine foods for the grey, adding important minerals to the diet. Head lettuce provides practically no food value. Provide the grey with a mineral block or cuttlebone and a good gravel mixture. Ask for one pound of small size grit, one pound small size crushed granite, one pound crushed oyster shell and one-quarter pound crushed charcoal. Mix these four ingredients together and sprinkle a little table salt into the gravel cup when you change it once a month. Even if the bird has not emptied the cup, it is advisable to change the mixture periodically. If you cannot obtain crushed charcoal, do not use charcoal briquettes or activated charcoal made for fish tank filters. In so doing, you will poison your bird. Better to do without charcoal.

Scrub the water cup daily with hot water and soap. Add a vitamin supplement to the water every day, not once or twice a week. These supplements are available at petshops. This may seem like a great deal of vitamin supplements, but remember that you are keeping a bird in captivity and may possibly be omitting something from the diet that wild birds eat

Opposite: A natural, healthy diet is an essential part of the African grey's life. Although seed is the basic staple, other items must be added to the diet. Many birds enjoy peanuts, sunflower seeds, and various fruits and vegetables. Get to know your pet's likes and dislikes by experimenting with different foods.

every day. Vitamin supplements have been used for many years with African greys and other parrot-type birds and have kept them in tip top condition, with the incidence of illness truly minimal.

Do not overfeed your pet grey parrot. A clipped bird does not require as many calories as a flighted one and may become overweight, endangering its health. There is no need to feed the bird twice a day unless it finishes all that you have given it in morning and is still hungry. If this is the case, go ahead and feed it a bit more in the afternoon. Experiment with the amount of food until you find that the bird is leaving some in the cup untouched. You will soon discover just how much feed it takes to

African greys in the wild find their own nutrition. It is, therefore, the duty of the owner of a captive parrot to try to duplicate the natural diet of the African grey.

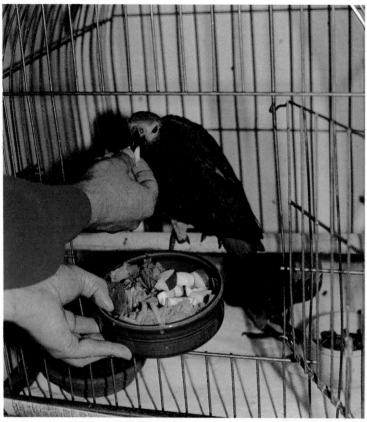

Variety is important in the African grey's diet, as it will help keep the bird healthy and interested in life.

keep your bird happy and at a good weight. Be flexible with the food. In the cold weather, birds tend to eat more than in the hot weather, and they probably increase their intake of food while molting. As the bird's physiological needs change, so will its need for nourishment. If you find that your bird is requiring a great deal of food and losing weight at the same time, seek the advice of a competent vet. You should get to know your bird as an individual. Like people, some tend to be thinner than others, but you should be aware of your bird's weight at all times to protect its health.

Clean the bird cage periodically with plain water. Sponge off the wire and scrub the bottom and grill. You may want to spray the cage with a commercial bird bug spray, but housepets rarely have lice or mites. Cedar shavings in the bottom of the cage instead of paper or sand help prevent bug infestation.

Give the bird a shallow dish of warm water to bathe in or see whether it enjoys being misted. Some greys love misting with warm water, spreading out their wings and ruffling up their feathers to catch every drop. Others show real displeasure and fear at the sight of the misting bottle. It is best to allow the grey to choose its own method of bathing. Some birds like to bathe every day. If this is the case, fine. In the wild, birds bathe often. In the very cold climates, it is better to forego the daily bath. Let the bird bathe early in the day to be sure that it dries completely before sundown.

Once your bird is very tame, you will probably think of taking it out to your favorite park or beach or over to a friend's house. Taking

Below: Your pet African grey parrot will live a long, happy life if it is given proper living conditions. *Opposite:* The cage or aviary must be cleaned periodically if the bird is to remain free of parasites.

A landing perch is a useful produ*
easily attaches to the top of a cage, and
lows a bird to sit unconfined for hours. A
able at pet shops everywhere. Photo cour
of Hagen. **Below:** Vitamin supplements ar
important part of your pet's diet. They are a
able in a variety of forms, such as powde
tablets, which make it easier to administer.
the clerk at your local pet store to help
choose which is best for your bird. Photo c
tesy of Hagen.

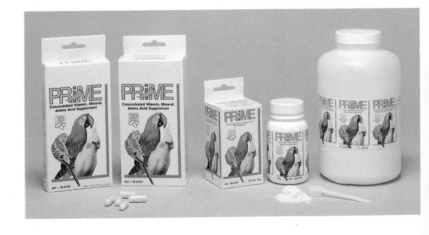

Above: *Spray Millet is enjoyed by many birds, from canaries and finches to the larger parrot-like birds. This nutritious treat is available at your local pet store in different quantities for your convenience. Photo courtesy of Hagen.*
Below: *Mineral and tonic blocks provide your bird with the required amount of minerals and calcium that it may not receive from its daily diet. They are available from your local pet store and are designed to attach easily to all cages. Photo courtesy of Hagen.*

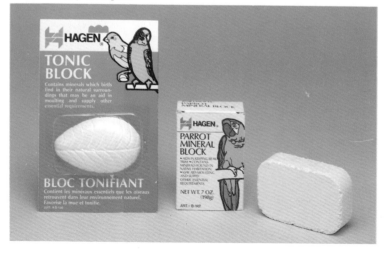

the bird to a public recreation area can be dangerous because of the dogs that will undoubtedly be present with their owners. In any event, be certain not to keep your bird out in the sun too long or it will become overheated and dehydrated. Bring along fresh drinking water. Keep the bird away from tall trees that it would be likely to climb. Leave the bird at home on cold, windy and rainy days. In the car, keep it out of the air conditioning draft and away from open windows. Better yet, don't open the windows. If you want to take the bird to a friend's house for the day, bring along its

African grey parrots have much higher rates of metabolism than do people. Therefore, never expect your bird to go without food for long periods of time.

African grey parrots should be housed in an area where the air is clean and free from smoke and drafts.

stand. Your bird deserves to be as comfortable as you are.

When going on a vacation, you can take your pet with you if the situation is right. If you plan to leave it in a hotel room while you sightsee, you would be better off leaving it at home with a friend. It is advisable to board the grey with someone that it knows, or at least in a private home, rather than a pet shop.

Use your common sense when giving the grey edible treats. It may like pizza and beer, but these are not good foods for it to eat. Cookies, cake, ice cream and other "goodies" are just not good bird food. Cheese (in moderation) is good bird food.

Opposite and above: You can train your African grey to climb on a treadmill created by your hands. Birds enjoy this sport, and it serves to build confidence between the trainer and the bird.

There are a few useful first aid preparations that you should purchase and keep on hand in case of an emergency. Most of these are available at the drug store. Buy some hydrogen peroxide, antiseptic powder, Mercurochrome and petroleum jelly at the pharmacy. Ask your pet shop to get some styptic powder for you if the shop doesn't stock it already. Use the peroxide as a cleansing agent for wounds and to stop minor bleeding. Sprinkle the antiseptic powder on cuts after treating with hydrogen peroxide. Petroleum jelly is a good salve to use on sore spots on the feet, legs and body, but try not to get it on the feathers. It is greasy and takes a long time to wear off. Styptic powder is great for stopping bleeding when you're clipping claws or when a bird breaks a blood feather or cuts itself.

If your bird has an accident, stay calm. You can't do it any good if you lose your composure. If it is a matter of a broken blood feather, wait for three to five minutes to see whether the blood will coagulate by itself. Whenever you grab a bird, its heart will beat faster and stronger, causing more and faster bleeding. If the blood stops flowing by itself, keep the bird quiet and warm until you can get to the vet for further treatment. Broken blood feathers may need to be pulled or they will continually bleed every time the bird bangs the broken spot. Do not attempt to pull the feather yourself unless you have had previous experience. Go to the vet or to an experienced bird handler.

If the bird breaks a claw or breaks off the tip of its beak, wait for a minute to see whether the bleeding will stop without first aid. If not, treat both injuries with styptic powder. Take a claw and dip it into the powder. For the broken beak, press the styptic powder into the bleeding tip. If bleeding continues, use more styptic powder and clean dry cotton to press against the spot. Hold it there for a few minutes to be sure that bleeding has stopped. Return the grey to its cage. Keep it warm and quiet, and leave it in for one or two days. Take the water out of the bird's cage overnight and return it the next morning.

You may come home from work or the store to find your grey twisted up in a piece of string from his cover or with a piece of wire from a toy. If its foot is tangled, move slowly and deliberately to keep from scaring the bird. You want to avoid having it yank on the leg, possibly causing further injury. Untangle and examine the bird. If the leg is swollen from having the circulation cut off, hold the

Opposite: *Knowing how to recognize illness and injury quickly can mean the difference between life and death for your African grey parrot.*

Taming your bird has advantages other than for the fun of it. Should you need to closely examine your grey for injury, such as this bird's puffy eye (below), having the bird accustomed to being fed from your hand (left) will make the job easier.

affected spot under warm running water for three to five minutes. Massage gently with your fingers. Paint the leg with Mercurochrome (not iodine) and put the bird in its cage to rest. Keep it warm and quiet. If you think the leg is broken, don't use the warm water treatment. Call your vet for advice.

Clean puncture wounds with hydrogen peroxide and sprinkle with antiseptic powder.

Have a veterinarian's phone number on hand in your telephone book so that you don't have to search for it should you need to call in a hurry. In case of accidents, act first, then call the vet for advice and follow-up care.

SICK BIRDS

There are a few things to watch for as signals of illness. If the bird's appetite suddenly drops off and it refuses to touch its feed, or if it stops whistling and sits with feathers ruffled instead of climbing around and playing as usual, you may suspect illness. Other indications are dull watery or red eyes and bright green, red-brown, all white or loose watery droppings. The bird's breathing may be heavy or irregular, and you may notice a wheezing sound as it inhales and exhales. The nasal passages may become clogged or runny. All of these symptoms indicate that something is wrong and that it is time to seek help from a qualified professional. Don't try to diagnose and treat

illness by yourself—it could mean your bird's life.

African greys can catch cold from bad weather or exposure to viral and bacterial agents. Colds can affect respiration and digestion. Greys can even catch sinus colds that result in red, swollen eyes and sore nasal passages. If left untreated, simple colds can develop into much more serious diseases like pneumonia.

When you take your grey to the vet for treatment of a cold, try to give the veterinarian some idea of the symptoms. Is the bird constipated or does it have diarrhea? Is it sneezing, coughing or wheezing? Has the bird stopped eating? Is it eating more than usual? These observations will help the veterinarian diagnose and treat the problem effectively. He may prescribe an antibiotic drug, and it is your responsibility to follow his prescription accurately and administer the medicine as ordered.

A sick bird must be kept quiet and very warm. This is where a hospital cage can come in handy. When the vet recommends a temperature of 90 to 95°F (32 to 35°C), that is just what he means. It may seem overly warm to you, but high heat is one of the most important factors in the successful treatment of many colds. Keep a check on the cage temperature with an accurate thermometer. If you are worried about dehydrating the bird, place a small dish of

A quartet of African grey parrots in an aviary. It is especially important that sick birds be separated from the rest of their colony, as illness can spread very quickly in birds.

water on the cage bottom to keep the cage humidified. Provide the bird with ample amounts of drinking water and feed. If the grey refuses to eat its normal feed mixture, give it plenty of whatever it will eat. Your vet can supply appetite stimulants when necessary.

Do not suspect your bird of having psittacosis if it becomes ill.

If your bird came from a reliable source and has been healthy in the past, it is extremely unlikely that it has psittacosis. Psittacosis is a respiratory disease that is caused by rickettsiae. It also affects animals other than birds but is very rare in a well fed, cleanly maintained household pet. The United States Department of Agriculture guards against

Opposite, top left: If you must handle or capture your African grey parrot for any reason, one of the better techniques involves the use of a towel. Quietly approach the grey and use the towel much like a bullfighter would use his cape. *Opposite,* **top right:** Then carefully drop the towel over the top of the grey and quickly but gently grasp the bird behind the head. *Opposite,* **bottom:** The author with two of her pets. The towel technique can be used for almost all birds. *Above:* During the clipping of the bird's feathers, you must be especially careful not to cut any blood feathers, which are feathers that are still growing.

psittacosis infection by requiring that all birds entering the U.S. go through a quarantine process. Samples are taken from the birds while in quarantine and are examined for both psittacosis and the exotic Newcastle disease. Only birds that check out as free from these diseases are allowed to leave the quarantine area. For this reason, you should never purchase a grey that may have been smuggled into the country. You not only take the risk of buying a sick bird, but you may also be endangering yourself and all those around you, man and animal alike.

Whenever you feel that your bird is ill, seek the advice of your veterinarian. Do not call him for every sneeze. All birds sneeze when they get dust in their noses, like people. Use your common sense. If you are concerned because the grey sneezes often, has a discharge from the nose or eyes, stops eating or continues to eat but loses weight, definitely call the vet.

Birds molt heavily once a year. They continually lose feathers and replace them. When a grey parrot loses too many feathers (enough to cause a bare spot) or begins to chew its feathers, you must take action. Check the diet. If the diet is wrong, correct it. Offer the bird fresh branches to chew. Be certain that the minerals in its dish are fresh. If not, replace them. If the mineral block or cuttlebone is old, replace it. Pay more attention to the grey parrot. Feather plucking or chewing may be the result of anxiety, frustration or loneliness.

The clipped wing may develop lumps when new feathers begin to grow. This happens because damage to the feather follicles has occurred. The new feathers cannot push through the skin layer that has grown over the follicle openings. The lumps are actually ingrown feathers. The feathers continue to grow into the wing because they cannot emerge from the damaged follicle openings.

Ingrown feathers must be extracted by a veterinarian or someone with a great deal of experience in removing such feathers. If the follicle can be reopened by the feather's extraction, a new feather may grow in the future. Sometimes when damage is severe, feathers will never grow from that follicle again.

Tumors can occur anywhere on the bird's body. Many can be removed surgically by the vet or can be cauterized. If you discover a lump on your bird, take him to the vet for examination. Without treatment, a tumor could grow and shorten your bird's life. With treatment, most birds can expect to live on in good health. There are instances of cancerous tumors in birds, but they are not prevalent. Do not conclude that your bird has cancer if a tumor

Whenever you feel that your African grey parrot may be ill, do not hesitate to call your veterinarian. The more quickly the vet can diagnose the problem, the better the bird's prognosis will be.

appears on its body.

Lameness and sore feet may be a problem for both young and old African greys. Birds that have wintered in outdoor aviaries can develop arthritis or rheumatism. Although they sleep with one foot drawn up into the feathers, the other foot has to remain on the perch. Continous exposure to extreme cold is not recommended. A grey may begin to favor one foot over the other and may begin to limp around the cage. Examine your bird. Is one foot warmer than the other? Is the sore foot very cold to the touch? Are there any wounds (old or new), raw spots or splits in the skin?

Clean wounds with hydrogen peroxide and dress with antiseptic salve. Don't cover the wound with a bandage. The bandage will bother the grey who will remove it. If your bird has gone lame, see the vet. If the toes on one foot curl

Lameness and sore feet are serious problems for birds (below and opposite). If you notice that one of your bird's feet is warmer than the other, consult your veterinarian immediately.

up and don't seem to grip the perch satisfactorily, keep the bird warm and quiet until you can get to the doctor.

Shock can occur when a bird flies into a window or wall head first or is badly injured some other way. The bird remains very still and may make crying, growling sounds. Usually a bird in shock is very docile and can be picked up without any struggle. Check to see that the bird is breathing. Wrap it up in a small cloth and place it in a very warm spot. This is when a hospital cage comes in handy. Use a small box when a hospital cage is not available. Ventilate the box with air holes, but remember that you want to keep the bird's movement and vision restricted. If the bird seems to come out of shock quickly, you should still give it plenty of warmth, quiet and rest for at least a day or two. If the shock is very serious, call the vet; don't drag the bird over. If the shock is a result of a wound or a broken limb, you may have to go to the vet. For your bird's sake, remain calm. Wrap the bird up in a towel and try to keep it as quiet and warm as possible on the ride over. Do not continually look at the bird to see how it is doing. You want to handle a bird in shock as little as possible.

Concussion resembles shock and should be treated the same way. Concussion usually occurs as a result of the bird's flying head first into a hard object. As a good

bird owner, you must protect it from such accidents by giving it a safe place to fly in. Use your common sense.

Female grey parrots may surprise you by laying eggs even though they have never been exposed to another bird. This is no problem as long as the diet is correct and well balanced. Egg production causes a strain on the bird's system, and good diet is imperative at these times. If a bird becomes eggbound, you must treat the condition. When a bird is eggbound, it is trying to pass an egg but is unable to do so. The musculature of the oviduct may be restricted in some part, or perhaps the bird is too weak to push the egg out. Give the bird plenty of heat by placing it in a small box that is easily heated up. First place two or three drops of mineral or vegetable oil on the vent. Be sure not to squeeze the grey. If the egg breaks inside the bird, it could be fatal. An experienced vet could push the egg out if the heat treatment doesn't work, but try heat and oil first. If the egg doesn't pass in a reasonable amount of time, see the vet. Eggbinding is usually a result of poor diet and insufficient vitamin and mineral supplements. Check the diet and adjust when necessary. Remember that eggbinding can also be caused by a lack of exercise. Give your grey plenty of time and space to exercise.

Whenever two or more birds are kept together, keep an eye out for plucked feathers. A disturbed bird may be plucking out its own feathers or those of other birds. Such behavior is a serious problem.

Above: Some pet shops have aviaries in their display areas. Such aviaries allow a potential buyer to become familiar with a parrot before its purchase. **Opposite, top:** Your local pet shop will usually provide you with a special box in which to take your bird home. Such a box will later be useful for transporting the bird to the vet or for other outings. **Opposite, bottom:** Commercial remedies for respiratory ailments in birds are available at pet shops everywhere. Photo courtesy of Hagen.

Breeding

Many people expect that if they put two grey parrots together they will breed and rear young. This expectation is usually fruitless, as the African grey is not one of the easier parrots to breed in captivity. Some aviaries are indeed blessed with fertile, prolific greys, but others await season after season for the first successful brood.

There are some basic principles to follow when attempting a breeding experiment. Give the birds a large flight cage and plenty of privacy. Use an enriched diet. Give supplements to the diet, both vitamins and minerals. The nest box can have a few different designs, so use the one that best suits your needs. The grandfather clock style of nest box is often preferred by the greys because it gives a great deal of privacy and resembles an old decayed tree trunk on the inside. The grandfather clock style nest box should be from four to six feet high, one foot wide, and one foot deep. The entrance hole should be about five inches in diameter (the greys will chew out more if they desire) and approximately ten inches from the top of the box. Use wood shavings (pine or cedar) to fill the box. Leave about 1½ feet of space between the top of the shavings and the entrance hole.

SEXING THE BIRDS

There are many theories on how to sex the grey parrot. The shape of the head and eyes, general size and bill construction are very unsatisfactory as accurate methods, so these ideas will not be related here. Recently, a method of surgical sexing has been developed in which a small incision is made and an endoscope is inserted into the bird's body cavity to observe the internal structures. This is a sure test for sexing parrots, but it may not appeal to every bird owner, as there is some risk involved in any surgical procedure. Should you be fortunate enough to obtain a few greys, place them all together in a large aviary and observe their behavior. When birds of both sexes are present and of breeding age, it is likely that they will pair off and save you the trouble of attempting to accurately sex them. When you observe one bird feeding another fairly consistently, meanwhile keeping away all other birds, you probably have a pair.

One further method of sexing grey parrots deserves mention. Sexing by fecal sampling, although less accurate than the surgical method, at least cannot harm the bird in any way. The feces are examined in the laboratory for hormone and steroid content and are then compared to

Opposite: Artist's rendering of a grey parrot in the wild. Breeding African greys in captivity is not easy, but it is possible if the right conditions are met.

Opposite: *It is almost impossible to sex an African grey parrot by looking at it. Many people, however, believe that a male grey is a better talker than a female.* **Above:** *Never choose to breed an African grey unless you are sure that its health and condition are excellent.*

a chart of the feces from known males and females. Analyses can vary, depending on whether or not the birds are in breeding condition, age, health and other factors. For more information on fecal sampling, write to the zoos with large bird collections.

MATING AND WAITING

Once you have the proper equipment—a pair of grey parrots with a well-balanced diet—you are ready to begin waiting. Waiting is one of the more familiar activities of a bird breeder. Waiting for the birds to show interest in the nest box, waiting for the eggs to be laid, waiting for the eggs to hatch and for sounds of feeding to come from the box. Finally, you must wait for the babies to emerge from the box with their first feathers.

Even then you must wait for the babies to be weaned before you can safely separate them from the parents. The process of incubation takes approximately 3½ weeks and is carried out solely by the hen. There is variation from pair to pair. Some greys take barely 21 days to hatch their young, while others may take as long as a month. Once the babies hatch, they will remain in the nest box for almost three months before poking their heads out to survey the outside world. About two weeks after leaving the box, the babies should begin to pick up and crack seed for themselves.

Once they are fairly independent and you do not observe the parents feeding the young, it is safe to remove them to a separate cage.

The pair may hatch out two to four chicks, which are covered with soft grey down. The hen remains with the young while the cock makes frequent trips to the feed dishes to keep the feeding hen well supplied with food for the chicks. By the second week the cock will join the hen in feeding the young, but at night the hen alone broods the chicks. This activity will continue for at least two months, after which the hen may begin roosting outside the box with the cock.

When they leave the nest box, young African greys look almost exactly like the adults, except for a few differences. Their eyes are black instead of yellow, and the plumage is slightly darker grey than the parents' plumage. The red feathers of the tail are a duller shade of red and often tipped with black. After the first heavy molt, these differences are no longer apparent.

You may want to hand-feed the young birds, or you may have to if the parents fail in this duty. Whenever possible, it is best to let the parents rear their young. When you must hand-rear the young, try to duplicate the diet that the parents would normally feed.

Index

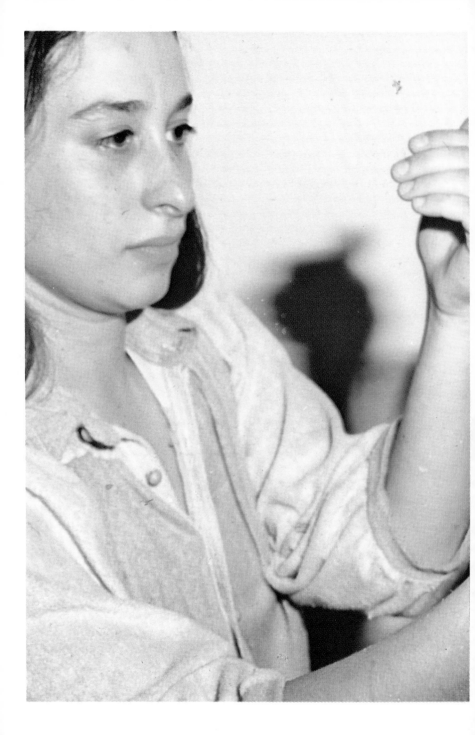

TRAINING AFRICAN GREY PARROTS
KW-025